Gregor the Overlander

A Novel Study

Copyright © 2010 by Jane Kotinek. All rights reserved.

ISBN: 13: 978-1470108021   ISBN-10: 147010802X

The classroom teacher may reproduce copies of materials in this book for classroom use only. The reproduction of any part for an entire school or school system is strictly prohibited. No part of this publication may be transmitted, stored, or recorded in any form without permission from the author.

Table of Contents

Page	Content
3	Introduction
4-8	Vocabulary List with activities and worksheets
9-12	Chapters 1 – 4 Questions
13	Essay: Connecting with Character
14-18	Chapters 5- 9 Questions
19	Essay: Text to Self Connection
20-24	Chapters 10- 14 Questions
24	Essay Question: Text to Self Connection
25-26	Venn diagram with essay
27-30	Chapters 15- 18 Questions
30	Essay: Text to World Connection
31	Character Chart
32-33	Character Trait Chart with Textual Proof
34-37	Chapters 19-22 Questions
38	Essay: Prediction
39-42	Chapters 23- 27 Questions
43	Internal/External Conflicts Chart
44	Analyzing Cause and Effect Activity
45	Analyzing the Title Activity
46	Analyzing the Theme Activity
47	Character Analysis Activity
48-49	Plot Diagram with Plot Summary Activity
50-66	Answer Keys to Novel Study Questions and Vocabulary Activities
67-80	Three multiple choice quizzes with Answers

Introduction

Gregor the Overlander by Suzanne Collins

This is the first book in the Gregor the Overlander series by Suzanne Collins.

The story begins after Boots, Gregor's two-year-old sister, falls into a shaft connected to the laundry room in their apartment complex. Gregor, in an effort to save his sister, jumps in after her. Together they arrive in a land like nothing they have seen before. They encounter giant cockroaches, bats, spiders, and rats. The people, fortunately, are human although nothing like Gregor has seen above ground.

After meeting some of the people of Regalia, Gregor realizes his father may be in the Underland. Through the Prophecy of Bane, it is believed Gregor is the warrior mentioned. He and a select few must travel through the Underland on a quest that will test everything they know and believe. Thus begins Gregor's quest to find his father.

The journey begun by Gregor, Boots, and the Underlanders will challenge their strength, friendship, and trust.

Vocabulary List

adamant	clustered	frail	implied	lucid
alliance	elated	frantic	intervened	prudent
annihilation	envious	glumly	intimidate	scampered
anxiety	existence	grudgingly	intricate	scurrying
arrogance	fatigue	immeasurable	lack	transpire

Vocabulary Activities

Directions: From the list below, choose TWO to complete for each set of vocabulary words. You may only do the same activity ONCE. Place an X on the line provided of the activity you have completed.

1. Write three synonyms and three antonyms for each word. _____

2. Create a crossword puzzle for the vocabulary words. _____

3. Write a short story using at least 15 of the words from the vocabulary list. _____

4. Write a sentence using each vocabulary word correctly. _____

5. Create a game (card or board game) using the vocabulary words and definitions. _____

6. Categorize the vocabulary words into three groups that clearly show the connection between the words. _____

7. Draw a picture that shows the meaning of the vocabulary word. Complete one picture for each vocabulary word. _____

8. Create a chart with the headings Setting, Character Trait, Emotional Description, and Action Description. Place the vocabulary words in the proper place in the correct column. _____

9. Find the sentences where the vocabulary words are used. Copy the sentences and replace the vocabulary word with a synonym. _____

Vocabulary Crossword Puzzle

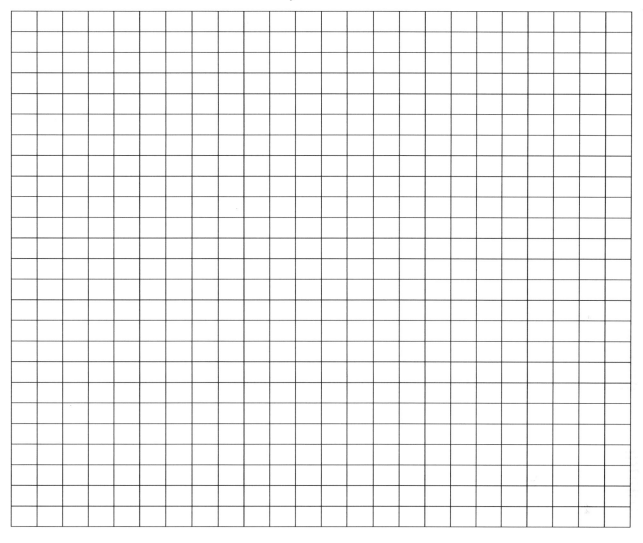

Directions: Provide numbered clues in the *across and down* sections below that match the words in the grid. Black out boxes that are not used with vocabulary word letters.

Across   **Down**

Gregor the Overlander

adamant	clustered	frail	implied	lucid
alliance	elated	frantic	intervened	prudent
annihilation	envious	glumly	intimidate	scampered
anxiety	existence	grudgingly	intricate	scurrying
arrogance	fatigue	immeasurable	lack	transpire

Directions: Use words from the vocabulary list above to complete the sentences below.

1. His _____ of energy prevented him from playing basketball.

2. The toddler _____ across the room to get the candy.

3. When she came out of the coma her memories were very _____.

4. I was _____ of my friends who were able to go to the dance.

5. I was suffering from _____ after I ran 10 miles.

6. The damage to the building was _____ due to the art work that was lost.

7. He was _____ in his denial of all charges against him.

8. She _____ admitted to her part in the prank.

9. No one knew what would _____ until the judge made her final decision.

10. The dogs were _____ around the food.

11. His _____ prevented him from being voted most popular.

12. Our _____ is dependent upon the amount of oxygen we receive.

13. His mother _____ after they started to fight.

14. The _____ of the dinosaurs is usually blamed on a huge comet.

15. "I don't care," he replied _____.

16. They were _____ as they looked for the clue.

17. She was thin and _____ when they found her.

18. The comments he made _____ he had found the secret room.

19. She refused to let the dog _____ her.

20. Tom's _____ rose the closer he came to test time.

21. The children were _____ to find the Easter eggs.

22. The _____ with the Europeans allowed them to win the war.

23. The pattern in the picture was very _____.

24. It was considered _____ of her to save her money for a rainy day.

25. Julia was _____ at the news she had received the scholarship.

Word Search

Word Search: Use the vocabulary list to complete the word search. Look for words horizontally, vertically, and backwards.

I	B	M	E	R	T	E	L	B	A	R	U	S	A	E	M	M	I
A	N	N	I	H	I	L	A	T	I	O	N	C	N	T	I	I	N
R	G	U	F	R	A	I	L	A	C	K	R	A	X	G	M	N	E
R	E	I	D	I	C	U	L	L	U	C	O	M	I	V	P	T	T
O	T	R	A	N	S	P	I	R	E	O	P	P	E	V	L	R	A
G	L	H	F	Y	I	F	A	T	I	G	U	E	T	T	I	I	D
A	E	X	I	S	T	E	N	C	E	T	C	R	Y	N	E	C	I
N	G	L	U	M	L	Y	C	L	U	S	T	E	R	E	D	A	M
C	I	T	N	A	R	F	E	U	S	T	M	D	N	D	E	T	I
E	L	A	T	E	D	E	N	V	I	O	U	S	R	U	G	E	T
G	R	U	D	G	I	N	G	L	Y	Y	I	U	E	R	D	S	N
G	N	I	Y	R	R	U	C	S	S	D	E	F	R	P	L	N	I
I	N	T	E	R	V	E	N	E	D	T	N	A	M	A	D	A	D

adamant   clustered   frail   implied   lucid

alliance   elated   frantic   intervened   prudent

annihilation envious   glumly   intimidate   scampered

anxiety   existence   grudgingly   intricate   scurrying

arrogance   fatigue   immeasurable lack   transpire

Gregor the Overlander
Part 1 The Fall
Novel Study Questions

Chapters 1

1. How would you describe Gregor's living conditions?

2. What happened to Gregor's father?

3. Why would Gregor's grandmother think it was her birthday in order to get a root beer?

4. Why were the clothes Gregor was washing grayish?

5. When was the last time Gregor felt happiness?

6. Why was this day significant?

7. What does Gregor think happened to his father?

8. How old is his sister, Boots?

9. What was Boots doing in the laundry room when Gregor found her?

10. What happened to her while she was looking into it?

___

Chapter 2

1. What was preventing Gregor and Boots from plummeting down the shaft?

___

2. What greeted Gregor after he fell to the floor of the cave?

___

3. What attracted the cockroaches to Boots?

___

4. Why do the cockroaches call Gregor *Overlander*?

___

5. Where did the cockroaches take Gregor and Boots?

___

6. What did Gregor see when he looked up into the sky?

___

Chapter 3

1. Describe the girl Gregor saw in the stadium.
   _____
   _____
   _____

2. What was Gregor's reaction to the girl when he met her?
   _____
   _____
   _____

3. How did Boots show she was smarter than the girl when she got the ball back from her?
   _____
   _____
   _____

4. Who was the girl?
   _____
   _____

5. Why did Luxa tell Gregor he needed to bathe?
   _____
   _____

6. What did the crawler's get from Luxa for Gregor and Boots?
   _____
   _____
   _____

Chapter 4

1. What was Gregor told when he said he needed to go home?
   _____
   _____
   _____

2. What did Luxa do when Gregor tried to escape from the stadium?
   _____
   _____

3. Why didn't the bats crash into each other when they were flying?

4. How did Gregor confuse the bats?

5. What do Gregor's actions tell us about him?

6. What is your impression of Vikus?

7. How did Gregor offend Vikus?

8. "Believe me, boy, by this time, every creature in the Underland knows you are here." This quote is an example of which type of figurative language? What does the quote mean?

9. What purpose do the small black moths serve to the Underland?

10. What is the name of the city Gregor and Boots are located in?

Essay Question: Gregor has shown quite a bit of his character especially when dealing with Luxa. Do you think his behavior has been appropriate given his circumstances? Explain your answer.

Chapter 5

1. What surprised Gregor about Regalia?

2. Who lives in the city?

3. How many gateways does the Underland have and where are they located?

4. Why are the gateways important to Gregor?

5. What did Gregor notice about the palace?

6. What was the reason for not having a door in the palace?

7. How does Gregor's personality differ from Boots's?

8. Why did Dulcet say Gregor was an important person?

9. Explain the area where Gregor took his bath.

10. What idea did the stream give Gregor?

Chapter 6

1. Why were Gregor's clothes burned?

2. Why was there no ceiling in the High Hall?

3. What does the feature in the High Hall show us about the relationship between the Underlanders and the bats?

4. How many people live in Regalia?

5. What does it mean to be "bonded" with a bat?

6. When discussing the crawlers, Henry states, "I would as soon bond with a stone." What does this quote tell us about Henry's character?

   _____
   _____
   _____

7. What important point does Vikus make concerning the crawlers?

   _____
   _____

8. How did the Underlanders get to the underground?

   _____
   _____

Chapter 7

1. What did Gregor find out about the water system from Dulcet?

   _____
   _____

2. Why did Gregor almost change his mind about escaping when he saw the actual river?

   _____
   _____

3. What did Gregor find by the river that he could use for his escape?

   _____
   _____

4. What did Gregor run into when he tried to get to the tunnel?

   _____
   _____
   _____

Chapter 8

1. After listening to the rats discussing him, what did Gregor realize the Underlander's were trying to do when they made him take a bath?

2. What did Gregor do that surprised and pleased the rats?

3. Why did the rats look stunned when Gregor thrust the torch at them?

4. Who saved Gregor from the rats?

5. Why couldn't Gregor flee from the fighting?

6. How did Gregor save Perdita?

7. What warning did Shed give to Gregor before he (Shed) died?

8. Why did the Underlanders burn the area where the fight had taken place?

Chapter 9

1. What did the Underlanders do to Gregor when they got him back to Regalia?
   _____
   _____

2. What did Luxa do to Gregor that angered Vikus?
   _____
   _____

3. Why did Vikus ask whether Gregor had fought or run during the battle?
   _____
   _____

4. What did Vikus show Gregor that he recognized immediately?
   _____
   _____

5. What does this information lead us to believe about Gregor's father?
   _____
   _____

Essay Question: Gregor has shown bravery, loyalty to Boots, and the ability to think quickly on his feet. How do you think you would have reacted if you were thrown into the same situation? Do you think you would display the same kind of bravery when faced with giant rats trying to kill you, or meeting up with huge cockroaches? Would you do anything differently? Explain your answer.

_____

_____

_____

_____

_____

_____

_____

_____

_____

_____

_____

_____

_____

_____

_____

_____

_____

_____

_____

_____

Part 2 The Quest
Novel Study Questions

Chapter 10

1. What did Vikus say happened to Gregor's father?

2. What rumor does Vikus tell Gregor?

3. What reason does Vikus give for his father's fate with the rats?

4. Where does Vikus take Gregor?

5. Why do the rats hate the Overlanders?

6. Who does Vikus believe the warrior mentioned in the prophecy is?

Chapter 11

1. What reasons did Gregor give to Vikus explaining why he isn't the warrior mentioned?

2. Who did Vikus say they would talk to about the contents of the prophecy?

3. What decision did the council reach in regards to whether Gregor was the warrior or not?

4. What did Luxa tell Gregor to do with Boots while they are on the quest?

5. What news did Keeda bring to the council?

Chapter 12

1. What did Vikus tell Gregor the war was about?

2. What things did Gregor take for his journey?

3. Besides the fact that Henry was going on the quest, why was his sister, Nerissa, crying?

4. What did Nerissa give Gregor right before they left for their quest?

5. What reason does Vikus give Gregor for the extra torches being lit around Regalia?

6. What is Solovet's purpose during the journey?

7. What is the metaphor Sandwich included in his prophecy, and what does it mean?

8. Why do they ask the bats permission?

9. What did Vikus tell Gregor he must do on the journey in regards to being a warrior?

10. How did Boots ruin Gregor's feeling of actually being the true warrior?

Chapter 13

1. Why didn't Vikus want Gregor at the war meeting with the bats?

2. Why should Vikus's response about Gregor not being in attendance during the war meeting put doubts in the minds of the bats?

3. What did Henry do to Boots that shocked Gregor?

4. What were the bats doing with Boots?

5. What did Gregor say to Luxa and Henry that offended them?

_____
_____
_____

6. When did Luxa and Henry become less kind to people?

_____
_____

7. Why didn't Gregor jump off the cliff when he was dared to do so by Luxa?

_____
_____
_____

Chapter 14

1. Upon meeting the crawlers, what did Boots do that pleased them?

_____
_____

2. Why was Temp surprised that Boots knew who he was?

_____
_____

3. What did Boots do at dinner time that no one else thought to do?

_____
_____

4. What does the reaction of the crawlers to Boots tell the reader?

_____
_____

5. Why did the crawler king refuse Vikus's request to join the quest?

_____
_____

6. How does Gregor defend the crawlers to Luxa and Henry after they made negative comments about the crawlers?

_____
_____

7. What question does Gregor ask Luxa during their discussion about the cockroaches that Vikus agrees she should ponder?

_____
_____
_____

8. What did Gregor see when he awoke?

_____
_____
_____

Essay Question: Answer Gregor's question to Luxa, "Do you think something deserves to die if it's not strong?" Defend your answer by supplying examples of why something should or should not die.

_____
_____
_____
_____
_____
_____
_____
_____
_____
_____
_____
_____
_____

Compare and Contrast: show the similarities and differences between Gregor and Luxa.

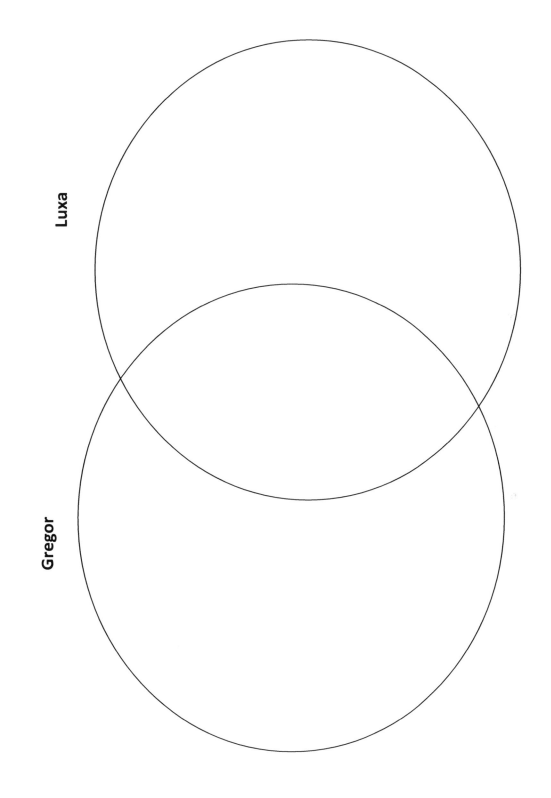

Compare/Contrast Activity

Directions: Using the Venn diagram completed on the previous page, write an essay comparing and contrasting Gregor and Luxa. Be sure you do not create a list in your essay. Use signal words for compare/contrast (First, for instance, compared to, etc.) to write your essay.

_____
_____
_____
_____
_____
_____
_____
_____
_____
_____
_____
_____
_____
_____
_____
_____
_____
_____
_____
_____
_____
_____
_____
_____
_____

Chapter 15

1. What did Vikus tell Gregor the crawlers were doing to Boots?

2. What is the name of the dance? Why is it important?

3. What did the crawlers tell the quest party the next morning? Why was this information important to those going on the journey?

4. Where is the quest party headed to next?

5. How were the crawlers able to protect their vast (huge) lands?

6. What did Vikus tell Temp and Tick after inviting them to dinner?

7. Who showed up after dinner?

8. What did the crawlers do to protect Gregor and Boots?

Chapter 16

1. Why did the spider stop spinning his web around Gregor and Boots?
   _____
   _____

2. As Gregor was dangling from the ceiling, what did he notice about the spiders that were different than the other creatures?
   _____
   _____

3. Why did Vikus tell Gregor it was good the rats had not seen Gregor?
   _____
   _____

4. Which spider came to greet the questers?
   _____
   _____

5. How did she communicate with Vikus?
   _____
   _____

6. What did she have done to the quest party?
   _____
   _____

Chapter 17

1. What did Gregor say to Vikus that cheered him up about their situation in the web?
   _____
   _____

2. Where did Gregor get more diapers?
   _____
   _____

3. Why did the crawlers refuse help from Solovet for their injuries?
   _____
   _____

4. How did the group plan to escape the web?

5. What did Gregor do as a distraction for the spiders?

6. What was Luxa doing to the web?

7. What happened when Luxa was near the top of the web?

Chapter 18

1. How did Gregor prevent the spider queen from biting Luxa?

2. What did Gregor say that made the Underlanders laugh for a long time?

3. What happens between Luxa and Gregor as they are talking?

4. Boots made two puddles of root beer for the crawlers and the bats. What does this action tell us about her?

5. Why are Mareth, Solovet, and Vikus leaving the quest?

6. Who was the guide Vikus had arranged to lead the group?
_____
_____

Essay Question: After reading the story you should be seeing a friendship developing between Boots and the Crawlers. Do you think this friendship is real? Could it happen in real life between two people with differing backgrounds, traditions, and way of doing thing? Give examples to prove your answer.

Gregor the Overlander

Character Chart

You have been introduced to many characters throughout the story. Fill in the chart with the characters from the story. You should add to the chart as the story progresses.

Character Name	Characteristics/description	Purpose in story
Gregor		Main Character. Protagonist.
Boots		
Luxa		
Vikus		
Henry		
Temp/Tick		
Ripred		
Ares		

Character Traits Chart

Directions: Each character in the book will have traits that separate them from others. Using textual proof, support your claims to the traits you believe each character possesses.

Gregor

Character Trait	Textual Proof	Page number

Luxa

Character Trait	Textual Proof	Page number

Character Traits Chart

Boots

Character Trait	Textual Proof	Page number

Vikus

Character Trait	Textual Proof	Page number

Henry

Character Trait	Textual Proof	Page number

Part 3 The Rat
Novel Study Questions

Chapter 19

1. What did the rat do when Henry attacked it with his sword?

2. What is the rat's name?

3. What did Gregor see in Ripred's eyes?

4. Why is Ripred helping the group on their journey?

5. Why did Vikus not tell anyone of his plan to use Ripred?

6. What is the relationship between Vikus and Luxa?

7. What were the reactions of Henry and Luxa to Vikus?

8. Why did Gregor decide to respond to Vikus even though he was angry at him?

Chapter 20

1. What was Henry's response when Gregor asked about the food?

2. Gregor's response to Henry shows growth in his character. What was his response to Henry, and how does it show growth?

3. What did Ripred tell Gregor most rats could do that surprised Gregor?

4. What do rats love?

5. Where did Ripred lead the group?

6. What did Gregor suggest the bats do in order to get through the tunnels quicker?

7. Why did Ripred lead the group through the foul smelling tunnel when he didn't need to do so?

8. What did the bats sense?

9. What happened when the spinners entered the tunnel where the group was located?

Chapter 21

1. What did Ripred tell Gox to do rather than eat the food for the questers?

2. Why did the rats attack the spinners?

3. What was the single saddest thing anyone had ever said to Gregor?

4. How does one bond with a bat?

5. What happens if one breaks the vow?

6. What was wrong with Boots?

7. What did Gregor see when he awoke from sleep during the night?

Chapter 22

1. What did Gregor do to stop Ares?

2. What was Henry's reaction to Gregor's claim that Henry had tried to kill Ripred in his sleep?

3. What character trait does Gregor display during the Henry/Ripred incident?
   _____
   _____
   _____

4. What do Henry's actions tell us about him?
   _____
   _____

5. What order did Luxa give to Henry?
   _____
   _____

6. Why do rats have to gnaw all the time?
   _____
   _____
   _____

7. Who was waiting for the group when they entered the cavern?
   _____
   _____

8. What did Ripred do when Gregor turned to go after Boots?
   _____
   _____

9. What happened to Tick?
   _____
   _____

10. How many in the group have died so far?
    _____
    _____

Essay Question: Tick's action to protect and save Boots was very brave. Think about the way the Underlanders view the cockroaches. Do you think Tick's actions will or will not change the way the Underlanders view the cockroaches?

_____
_____
_____
_____
_____
_____
_____
_____
_____
_____
_____
_____
_____
_____
_____
_____
_____
_____
_____
_____

Chapter 23

1. What made Gregor cry?
   _____
   _____

2. What did Gregor feel for the roaches?
   _____
   _____

3. How did Temp react to Gregor crying?
   _____
   _____

4. When was the last time Luxa cried?
   _____
   _____

5. What message did Luxa want Gregor to tell Vikus if she did not make it back?
   _____
   _____

6. What did Ripred tell Gregor that lifted Gregor's spirits?
   _____
   _____

7. What did Gox make for the questers and why?
   _____
   _____

8. What did the questers find in the pit?
   _____
   _____

Chapter 24

1. What was wrong with Gregor's dad?

2. What did the group discover concerning Henry's activities?

3. What was Luxa's response to Henry when she said she would die if she didn't join him?

4. Who showed up to capture the quest party?

5. Who did King Gorger kill?

6. Who is "the last to die" according to the Prophecy?

7. What did Gregor do when he got to the cliff?

Chapter 25

1. While Gregor was falling among the rats who did he see?

2. Who saved Gregor while he was falling?

3. What did Ares tell Gregor?

4. What is wrong with Luxa?

5. Why did Gregor ask Temp what they should do?

6. What happened to Gregor's dad at the waterfall?

7. What did Gregor's dad do to figure out which way to go?

8. What did Gregor see as they approached Regalia?

9. What gesture broke Luxa from her trance?

Chapter 26

1. What did Mareth tell Gregor?

2. What did Luxa tell Gregor when she was in his room?

3. What did Gregor do after Luxa told him?

4. What did Gregor do to prove he trusted Ares?

5. After his act with Ares, what challenge did Gregor make to the crowd?

Chapter 27

1. Why did the rats let Gregor's dad live?

2. What gift did Vikus give Gregor?

3. What is the gift Gregor is actually seeking?

4. What did Luxa tell Gregor after he said he would probably be grounded when he finally returned home?

5. Why is Gregor concerned about the Prophecy of Bane?

6. Where did Gregor and his family come out from the Waterway?

7. What did Gregor say when he entered the kitchen?

Internal/External Conflicts

Directions: There are many conflicts occurring within the story. Complete the chart below to demonstrate your understanding of the conflicts taking place in the novel. Put your choice of a conflict occurring in the story in the last box.

Conflict	Explanation of Conflict
Gregor vs. himself	
Gregor vs. Luxa	
Gregor vs. Getting home	
Gregor vs. His father	
Underlanders vs. Crawlers	

Cause and Effect Activity

Directions: Complete the cause and effect relationships listed below.

Cause	Effect
Gregor and Boots fall through the air duct.	
	Luxa and the group do not trust Henry as much as before the incident.

Essay Question: Explain how the cause/effect relationships move the story along.

_____
_____
_____
_____
_____
_____
_____
_____

Analyzing the Title Activity

Directions: An author chooses the title of their novel for a specific reason. Evaluate the title of the novel and explain why it is or is not a good title.

1. Does the title have a specific meaning to the book? If so, what is the meaning?

    _____
    _____
    _____
    _____

2. In the case of this novel, who or what does the title apply to?

    _____
    _____

3. Create a different title for the novel. Why do you think your title would/would not be a better title?

    _____
    _____

4. Comparing your title with the original, why is the original title better or worse than your choice?

    _____
    _____
    _____
    _____

Analyzing Theme Activity

Directions: Discuss the theme or themes of the story.

Theme: A general idea or message normally concerned with life, human nature, or society the author is trying to relay to the reader. A theme is usually a universal idea (love vs. hate, loyalty vs. disloyalty, fairness) that is not stated directly by the author rather it is understood by the reader through the evidence provided in the storyline.

1. Brainstorm as many themes as you can for the story. Write them below.

   _____

   _____

   _____

   _____

2. Which theme idea do you feel is the most important to the story? Explain your answer.

   _____

   _____

   _____

   _____

3. Can there be more than one theme to a novel?

   _____

   _____

   _____

   _____

4. Of the themes you mention above, which one do you relate to the most and why?

   _____

   _____

Character Analysis Activity

Directions: The novel has provided extensive proof of each character's personality and traits. Choose a character you could identify with and explain why you felt a connection with that character. Be sure to include examples of the traits you claim they possess that drew you to them.

_____
_____
_____
_____
_____
_____
_____
_____
_____
_____
_____
_____
_____
_____
_____
_____
_____
_____
_____
_____
_____
_____
_____
_____
_____
_____

Plot Diagram

Directions: Starting at the beginning of the story, place the most important events in order on the plot diagram below.

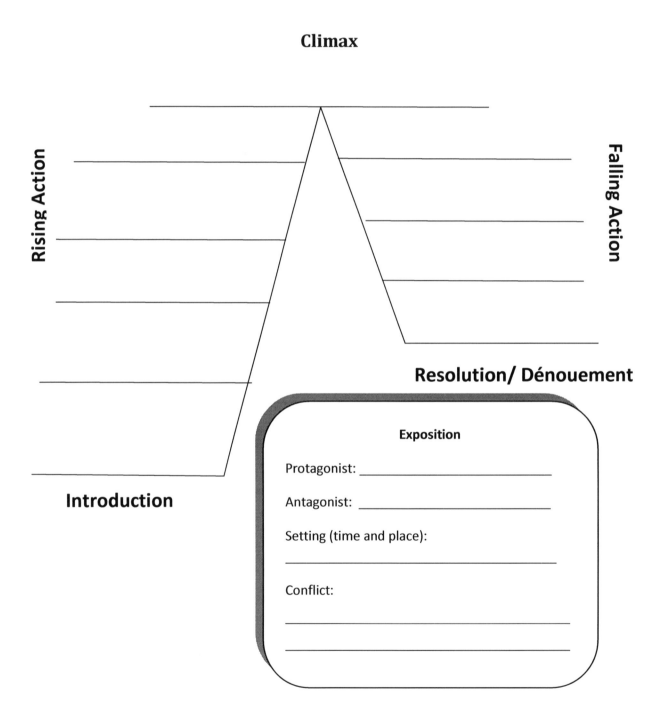

Plot Summary Essay

Directions: Using the Plot summary diagram, write an essay summarizing the plot of the story.

Answer Keys to Novel Study Questions and Vocabulary Activities

Gregor the Overlander
Vocabulary ANSWERS

Directions: Use the vocabulary list to complete the sentences below.

1. His __LACK__ of energy prevented him from playing basketball.

2. The toddler __SCAMPERED__ across the room to get the candy.

3. When she came out of the coma her memories were very __LUCID__.

4. I was __ENVIOUS__ of my friends who were able to go to the dance.

5. I was suffering from __FATIGUE__ after I ran 10 miles.

6. The damage to the building was __IMMEASURABE__ due to the art work that was lost.

7. He was __ADAMANT__ denial of all charges against him.

8. She __GRUDGINGLY__ admitted to her part in the prank.

9. No one knew what would __TRANSPIRE__ until the judge made her final decision.

10. The dogs were __CLUSTERED__ around the food.

11. His __ARROGANCE__ prevented him from being voted most popular.

12. Our __EXISTENCE__ is dependent upon the amount of oxygen we receive.

13. His mother __INTERVENED__ after they started to fight.

14. The __ANNIHILATION__ of the dinosaurs is usually blamed on a huge comet.

15. "I don't care," he replied __GLUMLY__.

16. They were __FRANTIC__ as they looked for the clue.

17. She was thin and __FRAIL__ when they found her.

18. The comments he made __IMPLIED__ he had found the secret room.

19. She refused to let the dog __INTIMIDATE__ her.

20. Tom's __ANXIETY__ rose the closer he came to test time.

21. The children were __SCURRYING__ to find the Easter eggs.

22. The __ALLIANCE__ with the Europeans allowed them to win the war.

23. The pattern in the picture was very __INTRICATE__.

24. It was considered __PRUDENT__ of her to save her money for a rainy day.

25. Julia was __ELATED__ at the news she had received the scholarship.

Word Search Answers

Word Search: Use the vocabulary list to complete the word search. Look for words horizontally, vertically, and backwards.

					E	L	B	A	R	U	S	A	E	M	M	I
A	N	N	I	H	I	L	A	T	I	O	N	C	N		I	I
R			F	R	A	I	L	A	C	K		A	X		M	N	E
R			D	I	C	U	L					M	I		P	T	T
O	T	R	A	N	S	P	I	R	E			P	E		L	R	A
G					F	A	T	I	G	U	E	T	T	I	I	D
A	E	X	I	S	T	E	N	C	E			R	Y	N	E	C	I
N	G	L	U	M	L	Y	C	L	U	S	T	E	R	E	D	A	M
C	I	T	N	A	R	F	E				D		D		T	I
E	L	A	T	E	D	E	N	V	I	O	U	S		U		E	T
G	R	U	D	G	I	N	G	L	Y				R			N
G	N	I	Y	R	R	U	C	S					P			I
I	N	T	E	R	V	E	N	E	D	T	N	A	M	A	D	A

Gregor the Overlander
Part 1 The Fall
Novel Study

Chapter 1

1. How would you describe Gregor's living conditions? *His family was obviously poor.*
2. What happened to Gregor's father? *He has disappeared.*
3. Why would Gregor's grandmother think it was her birthday in order to get a root beer? *In her youth it would have been a special treat that would have been expensive.*
4. Why were the clothes Gregor was washing grayish? *They were discolored due to age. The family could not afford new ones.*
5. When was the last time Gregor felt happiness? *Two years, 7 months, and 13 ago.*
6. Why was this day significant? *It was the day his father disappeared.*
7. What does Gregor think happened to his father? *He has died.*
8. How old is his sister, Boots? *She is two.*
9. What was Boots doing in the laundry room when Gregor found her? *She was looking into the old air duct where her ball had gone.*
10. What happened to her while she was looking into it? *She was sucked into it.*

Chapter 2

1. What was preventing Gregor and Boots from plummeting down the shaft? *A vapor was holding them steady.*
2. What greeted Gregor after he fell to the floor of the cave? *A huge cockroach, 4 feet tall.*
3. What attracted the cockroaches to Boots? *The smell of her dirty diaper.*
4. Why do the cockroaches call Gregor *Overlander*? *He comes from the land above them.*
5. Where did the cockroaches take Gregor and Boots? *A stadium.*
6. What did Gregor see when he looked up into the sky? *He saw bats flying with human riders.*

Chapter 3

1. Describe the girl Gregor saw in the stadium. *She had a very long braid with a gold band around her head. She was extremely pale and thin.*
2. What was Gregor's reaction to the girl he met? *He thought she was a show off with an attitude.*
3. How did Boots show she was smarter than the girl when she got the ball back from her? *Boots poked the girl in the eye which caused the girl to release the ball.*
4. Who was the girl? *Queen Luxa*

5. Why did Luxa tell Gregor he had to bathe? *It was unsafe for him to smell like an Overlander.*
6. What did the crawler's get for Gregor and Boots? *They received 5 baskets of grain from the humans.*

Chapter 4
1. What was Gregor told when he said he needed to go home? *He was told he could not go home.*
2. What did Luxa do when Gregor tried to escape from the stadium? *She blocked the exit using the bats.*
3. Why didn't the bats crash into each other when they were flying? *Due to echolocation- bats would emit a sound that would echo off something solid and they'd be able to tell where it was located.*
4. How did Gregor confuse the bats? *He caught them off guard when he sprinted for the exit without Boots. He then turned around and went back to her.*
5. What do Gregor's actions tell us about him? *He is a quick thinker, and he has an attitude-like Luxa.*
6. What is your impression of Vikus? *He is kind with a sense of humor.*
7. How did Gregor offend Vikus? *Gregor asked if they had killed the other Overlanders who had arrived in Underland.*
8. "Believe me, boy, by this time, every creature in the Underland knows you are here." This quote is an example of which type of figurative language? What does the quote mean? *Foreshadowing. Something is going to happen to Gregor that involves some or all of the creatures in the Underland that will not be good.*
9. What purpose do the small black moths serve to the Underland? *They are an early warning system.*
10. What is the name of the city Gregor and Boots are located in? *Regalia.*

Essay Question: Gregor has shown quite a bit of his character, especially when dealing with Luxa. Do you think his behavior has been appropriate given his circumstances? Explain your answer.

_____
_____
_____

Chapters 5
1. What surprised Gregor about Regalia? *It wasn't primitive. It was very beautiful.*
2. Who lives in the city? *The humans. The other creatures have their own "lands" they live in.*

3. How many gateways does the Underland have and where are they located? *There are 5 gateways. Two lead to Dead Land, 2 open into the Waterway, and one through New York City.*

4. Why are the gateways important to Gregor? *They are the only way he can get home.*

5. What did Gregor notice about the palace? *The sides were as smooth as glass, the lowest window opened 200 feet above ground. There was no door.*

6. What was the reason for not having a door in the palace? *"Doors are for those who lack enemies."*

7. How does Gregor's personality differ from Boots? *Gregor is more reserved. Boots is open, carefree, and she likes everyone immediately.*

8. Why did Dulcet say Gregor was an important person? *He was an Overlander.*

9. Explain the area where Gregor took his bath. *It was a pool with a hot stream running through it.*

10. What idea did the stream give Gregor? *He could get out of the palace using the stream that drains into the waterway.*

Chapter 6

1. Why were Gregor's clothes burned? *It was safer to burn them and get rid of their smell. "Ash leaves no scent."*

2. Why was there no ceiling in the High Hall? *The bats could enter the palace.*

3. What does this feature show us about the relationship between the Underlanders and the bats? *They have a mutual respect and working relationship with each other.*

4. How many people live in Regalia? *There are 3,000 residents.*

5. What does it mean to be "bonded" with a bat? *A union between a bat and a human that helps keep each other alive.*

6. When discussing the crawlers, Henry states, "I would as soon bond with a stone." What does his comment say about his attitude toward the crawlers? *He has little respect for the cockroaches.*

7. What important point does Vikus make concerning the crawlers? *Their (the Underlanders) continued existence is dependent upon the crawlers.*

8. How did the Underlanders get to the underground? *They came from England in the 1600s led by Bartholomew Sandwich. The Indians had shown them the Underland. Sandwich decided to live underground with 800 of his followers.*

Chapter 7

1. What did Grego find out about the water system from Dulcet? *It was dumped into the river below the palace. The river flowed into the Waterway.*
2. Why did Gregor almost change his mind about escaping when he saw the actual river? *The current was very fast and dangerous.*
3. What did Gregor find by the river that he could use for his escape? *He found a boat.*
4. What did Gregor run into when he tried to get to the tunnel? *He ran into huge rats.*

Chapter 8

1. What were the rats planning to do with Gregor and Boots? *They wanted to eat them.*
2. After listening to the rats discussing him, what did Gregor realize the Underlander's were trying to do when they made him take a bath? *They were trying to keep him alive.*
3. What did Gregor do that surprised and pleased the rats? *He spoke to them instead of whining or screaming in fear.*
4. Why did the rats look stunned when Gregor thrust the torch at them? *They saw his shadow and it meant something to them.*
5. Who saved Gregor from the rats? *The bats, Henry, Mareth, and Perdita saved Gregor.*
6. Why couldn't Gregor flee from the fighting? *He had no idea where he should go.*
7. How did Gregor save Perdita? *Gregor burned Fangor in the face with the torch which caused him to back up into Henry's sword.*
8. What warning did Shed give to Gregor before he (Shed) died? *He said the rats would hunt him down until they were all dead trying.*
9. Why did the Underlanders burn the area where the fight had taken place? *They wanted to get rid of the scent.*

Chapter 9

1. What did the Underlanders do to Gregor when they got him back to Regalia? *They tied his hands behind his back and made him a prisoner.*
2. What did Luxa do to Gregor that angered Vikus? *She slapped Gregor across the face. He also found out she was at the scene of the fight.*
3. Why did Vikus ask whether Gregor had fought or run during the battle? *He wanted to find out if Gregor ran in the face of danger.*

4. What did Vikus show Gregor that he recognized immediately? *The key chain Gregor had made for his father.*

5. What does this information lead us to believe about Gregor's father? *His father had been in the Underland and may still be alive.*

Essay Question: Gregor has shown bravery, loyalty to Boots, and the ability to think quickly on his feet. How do you think you react if you were thrown into the same situation? Do you think you would display the same kind of bravery when faced with giant rats trying to kill you, or meeting up with huge cockroaches? Would you do anything differently? Explain your answer.

_____
_____
_____
_____

Chapters 10

1. What did Vikus say happened to Gregor's father? *The rats had gotten him.*
2. What rumor does Vikus tell Gregor? *The rats have kept his father alive.*
3. What reason does Vikus give for his father's fate with the rats? *Gregor's father is a Science teacher who would know how to create bombs. The rats would want him to create bombs for them.*
4. Where does Vikus take Gregor? *He takes him to the room that contains the prophecies of Bartholomew of Sandwich. The prophecies are carved into the walls.*
5. Why do the rats hate the Overlanders? *The prophecy mentions that an Overland warrior will have something to do with their downfall.*
6. Who does Vikus believe the warrior mentioned in the prophecy is? *Gregor*

Chapter 11

1. What reasons did Gregor give to Vikus explaining why he isn't the warrior mentioned? *He was only 11 years old, and he wasn't a fighter.*
2. Who did Vikus say they would talk to about the contents of the prophecy? *The council.*
3. What decision did the council reach in regards to whether Gregor was the warrior or not? *They believed him to be the warrior.*

4. What did Luxa tell Gregor to do with Boots while they are on the quest? *He should take Boots with him on the quest.*

5. What news did Keeda bring to the council? *The rats were attacking Regalia.*

Chapter 12

1. What did Vikus tell Gregor the war was about? *It was the war mentioned in the prophecy.*

2. What things did Gregor take for his journey? *A flashlight with batteries, a hard hat with a light on it, and a can of root beer.*

3. Besides the fact that Henry was going on the quest, why was his sister, Nerissa, crying? *She was having recurring dreams that Henry would die.*

4. What did Nerissa give Gregor right before they left for their quest? *"The Prophecy of Gray" copied and carefully written on paper.*

5. What reason does Vikus give Gregor for the extra torches being lit around Regalia? *Only the humans need light, none of the other creatures in the Underland need it to see.*

6. What is Solovet's purpose during the journey? *She plans the attacks and figures out the amount of support they can expect from allies.*

7. What is the metaphor Sandwich included in his prophecy, and what does it mean? *"May bring us back light." The word light in the metaphor means life.*

8. Why do they ask the bats permission? *They need the bats permission to go to war.*

9. What did Vikus tell Gregor he must do on the journey in regards to being a warrior? *Gregor must make the other creatures believe he is the warrior mentioned in the prophecy.*

10. How did Boots ruin Gregor's feeling of actually being the true warrior? *She announced she needed a diaper change.*

Chapter 13

1. Why didn't Vikus want Gregor at the war meeting with the bats? *They would be discussing battle positions for the forces, not the efforts of the quest.*

2. Why should Vikus's response about Gregor not being in attendance during the war meeting put doubts in the minds of the bats? *If Gregor was the true warrior, shouldn't he be involved with the battle decisions?*

3. What did Henry do to Boots that shocked Gregor? *He threw Boots over the side of the cliff.*

4. What were the bats doing with Boots? *They were playing a game of catch with her by throwing her up in the air and catching her.*

5. What did Gregor say to Luxa and Henry that offended them? *He said the Underland was creepy.*

6. When did Luxa and Henry become less kind to people? *When the rats took their parents.*

7. Why didn't Gregor jump off the cliff when he was dared to do so by Luxa? *He was too afraid.*

Chapter 14

1. Upon meeting the crawlers, what did Boots do that pleased them? *She ran up to them with outstretched arms.*

2. Why was Temp surprised that Boots knew who he was? *She recognized him from when she first met him. This seldom happened with humans.*

3. What did Boots do at dinner time that no one else thought to do? *She invited Temp and Tick to dinner with the rest of the group.*

4. What does the reaction of the crawlers to Boots tell the reader? *The crawlers and Boots are developing a relationship with one another that hasn't happened with any other human before.*

5. Why did the crawler king refuse Vikus's request to join the quest? *He didn't want to upset the peace they had with the humans and the rats.*

6. How does Gregor defend the crawlers to Luxa and Henry after they made negative comments about the crawlers? *He tells them cockroaches have been around for 350 million years and humans for less than 6 million.*

7. What question does Gregor as Luxa during their discussion about the cockroaches that Vikus agrees she should ponder? *"Do you think something deserves to die if it's not strong?"*

8. What did Gregor see when he awoke? *The cockroaches were dancing around boots.*

Essay Question: Answer Gregor's question to Luxa, "Do you think something deserves to die if it's not strong?" Defend your answer by supplying examples of why something should or should not die.

_____
_____
_____
_____
_____
_____

Part 2 The Quest
Novel Study Questions

Chapters 15

1. What did Vikus tell Gregor the crawlers were doing to Boots? *They were honoring her in a manner most sacred and rare.*

2. What is the name of the dance? *The Ring Dance*

3. Why is it important? *It is a dance for the Chosen, who will give them time.*

4. What did the crawlers tell the quest party the next morning? Why was this information important to those going on the journey? *Temp and Tick would be joining them. According to the prophecy, they needed two crawlers to join their quest.*

5. Where is the quest party headed to next? *They are headed to the land of the spinners.*

6. How were the crawlers able to protect their vast (huge) lands? *There were thousands upon thousands of roaches.*

7. What did Vikus tell Temp and Tick after inviting them to dinner? *All were equal here.*

8. Who showed up after dinner? *Six rats intent on killing Gregor.*

9. What did the crawlers do to protect Gregor and Boots? *They filled up the tunnel with their bodies to prevent the rats from entering.*

Chapter 16

1. Why did the spider stop spinning his web around Gregor and Boots? *Gregor mentioned he knew Vikus.*

2. As Gregor was dangling from the ceiling, what did he notice about the spiders that were different than the other creatures? *They couldn't care less about Gregor or that he was the warrior mentioned in the prophecy.*

3. Why did Vikus tell Gregor it was good the rats had not seen Gregor? *He resembled his father.*

4. Which spider came to greet the questers? *Queen Wevox.*

5. How did she communicate with Vikus? *She rubbed her front legs over her chest to produce her voice.*

6. What did she have done to the quest party? *She had a 30 foot wall of web built to surround them.*

Chapter 17

1. What did Gregor say to Vikus that cheered him up about their situation in the web? *The spiders were going to eat Gregor before he mentioned his name?*

2. Where did Gregor get more diapers? *The spiders made him 2 dozens.*

3. Why did the crawlers refuse help from Solovet for their injuries? *They could heal themselves.*

4. How did the group plan to escape the web? *They planned to perform the coiler.*

5. What did Gregor do as a distraction for the spiders? *He taunted Boots with a cookie which caused her to scream loudly.*

6. What was Luxa doing to the web? *She was cutting it with her sword as she went around the web in circles.*

7. What happened when Luxa was near the top of the web? *Luxa was caught in another web.*

Chapter 18

1. How did Gregor prevent the spider queen from biting Luxa? *He sprayed root beer soda in her eyes.*

2. What did Gregor say that made the Underlanders laugh for a long time? *He asked if he should have a sword.*

3. What happens between Luxa and Gregor as they are talking? *They show a mutual respect by saying "thank you" and "sorry" to each other.*

4. Boots made two puddles of root beer for the crawlers and the bats. What does this say about her character? *She is compassionate and friendly.*

5. Why are Mareth, Solovet, and Vikus leaving the quest? *They are not mentioned in the prophecy.*

6. Who was the guide Vikus had arranged to lead the group? It was the *rat with a diagonal scar across his face that Vikus had knocked into the river.*

Essay Question: After reading the story you should be seeing a friendship developing between Boots and the Crawlers. Do you think this friendship is real? Could it happen in real life between two people with differing backgrounds, traditions, and way of doing thing? Give examples to prove your answer.

_____
_____
_____

Part 3 The Rat
Novel Study Questions

Chapters 19

1. What did the rat do when Henry attacked it with his sword? *The rat flicked his tail and knocked Henry's sword out of his hand.*

2. What is the rat's name? *Ripred*

3. What did Gregor see in Ripred's eyes? *He saw pain, danger, and intelligence.*

4. Why is Ripred helping the group on their journey? *He wants their help to overthrow the rat king, Gorger.*

5. Why did Vikus not tell anyone of his plan to use Ripred? *He knew they would be upset.*

6. What is the relationship between Vikus and Luxa? *She is his granddaughter.*

7. What were the reactions of Henry and Luxa to Vikus? *They turned their backs on him and would not speak to him as he left.*

8. Why did Gregor decide to respond to Vikus even though he was angry at him? *There were too many things he wished he's said to his dad but couldn't.*

Chapter 20

1. What was Henry's response when Gregor asked about the food? *He and Luxa were royalty and did not serve food.*

2. Gregor's response shows growth in his character. What was his response to Henry, and how does it show growth? *He said Henry and Luxa would get very hungry because he was not going to serve them. His self confidence and courage is increasing.*

3. What did Ripred tell Gregor most rats could do that surprised Gregor? *Most rats could read.*

4. What do rats love? *Themselves.*

5. Where did Ripred lead the group? *He led them into the tunnels.*

6. What did Gregor suggest the bats do in order to get through the tunnels quicker? *He suggested they ride the backs of Temp and Tick.*

7. Why did Ripred lead the group through the foul smelling tunnel when he didn't need to do so? *He wanted to cover the smell of them.*

8. What did the bats sense? *They sensed the presence of spinners.*

9. What happened when the spinners entered the tunnel where the group was located? *An orange spider with a brown spider entered. The brown spider told the group the gnawers had attacked their webs. The brown spider died.*

Chapter 21

1. What did Ripred tell Gox to do rather than eat the food for the questers? *He told Gox to eat the brown spider.*

2. Why did the rats attack the spinners? *Either King Gorger had launched a total Underland attack, or the rats found out two Overlanders were heading toward their land.*

3. *What was the single saddest thing anyone had ever said to Gregor?* When Luxa told him, "If you are not trying to hold on to time, you are not so afraid of losing it."

4. How does one bond with a bat? *It's a simple ceremony where both the bat and the human say a vow to one another.*

5. What happens if one breaks the vow? *The guilty one is banished to live alone in the Underland. Living alone would more than likely lead to death.*

6. What was wrong with Boots? *She was too quiet and her skin was clammy and cold.*

7. *What did Gregor see when he awoke from sleep during the night?* He saw Henry about to stab Ripred with his sword.

Chapter 22

1. What did Gregor do to stop Ares? *He jumped between the rat and the bat.*

2. What was Henry's reaction to Gregor's claim that Henry had tried to kill Ripred in his sleep? *He admitted his attempt to kill Ripred without feeling sorry.*

3. What character trait does Gregor display during the Henry/Ripred incident? *Gregor displayed bravely, loyalty, and leadership.*

4. What do Henry's actions tell us about him? *He lacks honor and cannot be trusted.*

5. What order did Luxa give to Henry? *He was to leave Ripred alone.*

6. Why do rats have to gnaw all the time? *Rats' teeth continue to grow throughout their lives. If they do not gnaw the lower teeth will grow into their skull.*

7. Who was waiting for the group when they entered the cavern? *There were about 20 rats waiting for them.*

8. What did Ripred do when Gregor turned to go after Boots? *He snagged his backpack and carried Gregor across the bridge.*

9. What happened to Tick? *He died saving Boots from the rats.*

10. How many from the group have died so far? *2*

Essay Question: Tick's action to protect and save Boots was very brave. Think about the way the Underlanders view the cockroaches. Do you think Tick's actions will or will not change the way the Underlanders view the cockroaches?

Chapter 23

1. What made Gregor cry? *Tick's sacrifice to save the life of Boots.*

2. What did Gregor feel for the roaches? *He felt an allegiance that would never fade.*

3. How did Temp react to Gregor crying? *She was honored by Gregor's reaction because it showed he cared about the crawlers.*

4. When was the last time Luxa cried? *When her parents died.*

5. What message did Luxa want Gregor to tell Vikus if she did not make it back? *She wanted Vikus to know she understood why he had left them with Ripred.*

6. What did Ripred tell Gregor that lifted Gregor's spirits? *His father was only an hour away.*

7. What did Gox make for the questers and why? *She made silk slippers so they could not be heard walking.*

8. What did they find in the pit? *Gregor's father.*

Chapter 24

1. What was wrong with Gregor's dad? *He was weak, frail, and he couldn't remember things due to the fever he had.*

2. What did the group find out Henry had done? *He had betrayed them by siding with the rats.*

3. What was Luxa's response to Henry when she said she would die if she didn't join him? *She said, "This is as good as any day, perhaps better."*

4. Who showed up to capture the quest party? *King Gorger.*

5. Who did King Gorger kill? *Gox*

6. Who is "the last to die" according to the Prophecy? *Gregor*

7. What did Gregor do when he got to the cliff? *He leaped.*

Chapter 25

1. While Gregor was falling among the rats who did he see? *Henry.*

2. Who saved Gregor while he was falling? *Ares, Henry's bat.*

3. What did Ares tell Gregor? *He did not know Henry was a traitor.*

4. What is wrong with Luxa? *She is in shock over Henry's betrayal.*

5. Why did Gregor ask Temp what they should do? *She was the only one left in the grou who wasn't hurt or in despair.*

6. What happened to Gregor's dad at the waterfall? *He came back to life after taking the medicine and remembered Gregor.*

7. What did Gregor's dad do to figure out which way to go? *He made a compass out of the needle and lodestone.*

8. What did Gregor see as they approached Regalia? *He saw the death of war.*

9. What gesture broke Luxa from her trance? *Her grandfather, Vikus, outstretched his arms to her.*

Chapter 26

1. What did Mareth tell Gregor? *She told him he had brought back the light.*

2. What did Luxa tell Gregor whe she was in his room? *She told him Ares was going to be banished because he had broken the bond.*

3. What did Gregor do after Luxa told him? *He burst into the council room to try to stop Ares from being banished.*

4. What did Gregor do to prove he trusted Ares? *He bonded with Ares.*

5. After his act with Ares, what challenge did Gregor make to the crowd? *He dared then to banish Ares.*

Chapter 27

1. Why did the rats let Gregor's dad live? *He told them he could make weapons they could use.*

2. What did Vikus give Gregor? *He gave Gregor Sandwich's sword.*

3. What is the gift Gregor is actually seeking? *Hope*

4. What did Luxa tell Gregor after he said he would probably be grounded when he finally returned home? *Not according to "The Prophecy of Bane."*

5. Why is Gregor concerned about the Prophecy of Bane? *He doesn't know if he is mentioned in it or not.*

6. Where did Gregor and his family come out from the Waterway? *Central Park in New York City.*

7. What did Gregor say when he entered the kitchen? *"We're home."*

Quizzes with Answers

Gregor the Overlander Part I Quiz

Name _____

Directions: Choose the best answer for the question.

1. How did Gregor and Boots get to the Underland?

    A. Through the waterway.

    B. Through the air duct in the laundry room.

    C. Through the waterway in Central Park.

    D. Through the air duct in Central Park.

2. What attracted the cockroaches to Boots?

    A. Her perfume.

    B. Her fantastic personality.

    C. The smell from her dirty diaper.

    D. The way she smiled at them.

3. Upon first meeting Luxa, what was Gregor's reaction to her?

    A. He thought she was arrogant.

    B. He liked her tremendously.

    C. He thought he had a crush on her.

    D. He liked the way she acted toward him.

4. What word would best describe Boots?

    A. Mean spirited.

    B. Glum

    C. Arrogant

    D. Carefree

5. Why are the gateways important to Gregor?

    A. They provide the hot water for the bath.

    B. They provide enough water for Regalia to live.

    C. They lead to the Underland.

    D. They lead to the Overland.

Gregor the Overlander

Part I Quiz

6. Why did the palace surprise Gregor?

    A. It had no doors.

    B. It was made of lodestone.

    C. It wasn't very pretty.

    D. It was small.

7. What does "bonded" mean as it is used in the story?

    A. Two humans are glued together for life.

    B. Two bats must protect each other until one or the other dies.

    C. A human and a bat protect each other until one or the other dies.

    D. A human and a bat feel a strong connection to each other and live together.

8. Why did Gregor find the bath to be very interesting?

    A. He was surprised they knew what soap was.

    B. He was interested to find a stream ran through it.

    C. He was surprised it looked so much like the one he had at home.

    D. He didn't find anything interesting about it.

9. Why were Boots and Gregor's clothes burned?

    A. They were badly damaged in the flight down.

    B. They were old and useless.

    C. They smelled of the Overland.

    D. They weren't made by the Underlanders.

10. What word best describes Henry?

    A. Leader

    B. Carefree

    C. Friendly

    D. Rude

Gregor the Overlander

Part I Quiz

11. When did the humans arrive to the Underland?

    A. 1600s

    B. 1800s

    C. 1700s

    D. 1900s

12. What did Gregor run into during his escape?

    A. Rats

    B. The forest

    C. Spinners

    D. The swamp

13. Gregor realized the Underlanders had he and Boots take baths to

    A. teach them a lesson.

    B. punish them for landing in underland.

    C. save their lives.

    D. be impressed by their water system.

14. What did Shed tell Gregor right before he died?

    A. The Spinners would get him eventually.

    B. He was bound to die in the Underland.

    C. The rats would hunt him down until they were all dead.

    D. He and Boots would never return to the Overland.

15. What did Luxa do that angered Vikus?

    A. She told him to mind his own business.

    B. She was involved in the fight to save Gregor.

    C. She reminded him that she was queen.

    D. She ignored his request to set Gregor free.

Gregor the Overlander
Part I Quiz

16. What do we know about Gregor's father?

    A. He had been in the Underland.

    B. He was dead.

    C. He died while trying to escape back to the Overland.

    D. He died while living with the crawlers.

17. How are the cockroaches viewed by Vikus?

    A. He holds nothing but contempt (immense dislike) for them.

    B. He hates them.

    C. He wishes they would go away and leave the people of Regalia alone.

    D. He believes Regalia needs then in order for them to exist.

18. The bats can best be described as

    A. Being a nuisance to Regalia.

    B. Being better than the humans because they can fly.

    C. Being equal to the humans.

    D. Being no better than the rats.

19. Which character trait does **not** apply to Gregor?

    A. Vicious

    B. Intelligent

    C. Brave

    D. Caring

20. You can infer from Henry's attitude toward the crawlers

    A. he regards them with respect and admiration.

    B. he likes them immensely.

    C. he finds them very intelligent and friendly.

    D. he has little respect for them.

Gregor the Overlander Part II Quiz

Name _____

Directions: Choose the best answer for the question.

1. Why would the rats keep Gregor's father alive?

    A. They thought he could get them to the Overland.

    B. They thought he could teach them to write.

    C. They thought he could make weapons for them.

    D. They thought they could get to Gregor, the warrior, through him.

2. What is the prophecy carved into the wall?

    A. It tells of the rats success against the humans.

    B. It tells of the outcome for the Underland.

    C. It shows how the bats will betray the Underland.

    D. It shows the outcome for the Overland.

3. What/who governs the people of Regalia?

    A. Vikus and Luxa

    B. The council

    C. The rats

    D. The bats

4. What did Gregor take on the journey?

    A. Medicine, flashlight, and root beer.

    B. Flashlight, hard hat, and sword.

    C. Flashlight, sword, and medicine.

    D. Flashlight, root beer, and a hard hat.

5. What recurring dream made Nerissa cry?

    A. The Underlanders were defeated by the rats.

    B. The crawlers became the new government.

    C. Her brother dying.

    D. Luxa dying during battle.

Gregor the Overlander
Part II Quiz

6. What is the meaning for the quote, "May bring us back light?"

   A. Life

   B. Light

   C. Liberty

   D. Luxury

7. What word would best describe the mood of the story?

   A. Humorous

   B. Glum

   C. Tense

   D. Jovial

8. What did Henry do to Boots that upset Gregor?

   A. He made fun of her.

   B. He teased her with a cookie.

   C. He told her she was as dumb as the crawlers.

   D. He threw her over the side of the cliff.

9. What reason did Luxa give to Gregor for not being afraid of falling?

   A. The end of life must come at some time.

   B. Only those who were afraid of death would be afraid of falling.

   C. The bats would catch him if he fell.

   D. A warrior must face his fears.

10. Why wouldn't Gregor jump off the cliff?

   A. He had already done it once.

   B. He wasn't dumb enough to try it.

   C. He knew there was no purpose to it.

   D. He was afraid.

Gregor the Overlander

Part II Quiz

11. What did Boots do that surprised and pleased the crawlers?

    A. She gave them a gift.

    B. She recognized them.

    C. She gave them a big hug.

    D. She smiled at them.

12. How does Boots keep surprising everyone?

    A. She is always well behaved.

    B. She doesn't throw tantrums.

    C. She is constantly thinking of everyone else's feelings.

    D. She acts like she is five.

13. What ceremony did the cockroaches perform for Boots?

    A. The Ring Dance

    B. The Crawler Ceremony

    C. The Friendship Dance

    D. The Circle of Friends dance

14. The crawlers could best be described as

    A. protective

    B. unintelligent

    C. lazy

    D. unfriendly

15. Why was it a good thing the rats had not seen Gregor?

    A. He would have scared them to death.

    B. They would have known he was only 10.

    C. They would have seen that he looked like his dad.

    D. They would have laughed at the "warrior."

Gregor the Overlander

Part II Quiz

16. What did Gregor do to save Luxa from the spider queen?

    A. He used Luxa's sword to stab the queen.

    B. He cut through the web the queen had sprayed over Luxa.

    C. He punched the queen in her stomach causing her to drop Luxa.

    D. He sprayed root beer in her eyes.

17. What words best describe Boots?

    A. Friendly and compassionate.

    B. Friendly and vicious

    C. Vicious, but kind

    D. Head-strong and mean

18. Who would be the groups guide?

    A. A spinner

    B. A crawler

    C. A rat

    D. A bat

19. How do Luxa and Gregor finally become friends with one another?

    A. They fight it out until one of them wins.

    B. They admit their wrong doings and say "thank you" to one another.

    C. Luxa lets Gregor ride her bat.

    D. Gregor lets Luxa wear the hard hat.

20. According to the prophecy, how many will die during the quest?

    A. 1

    B. 2

    C. 3

    D. 4

Gregor the Overlander

Quiz Part 3

Name _____

1. What does Henry's attempt to assassin Ripred tell us about him?

    A. He is loyal to the Underlanders.

    B. He is concerned about Luxa

    C. He wants the questers to succeed on their journey.

    D. He cannot be trusted.

2. Who prevented Gregor from going after Boots on the bridge?

    A. Ripred

    B. Temp

    C. Luxa

    D. Henry

3. What would happen to the human or bat if they broke the bonding vow?

    A. They would be banished from the Underland.

    B. They would have to find a new partner.

    C. They would be annihilated.

    D. Nothing would happen to either.

4. Why did the spinners join the quest?

    A. They decided it was in their best interests to keep an eye on Gregor.

    B. They didn't trust the humans.

    C. The rats had attacked them.

    D. The decided it was time they intervened.

5. What did Gregor suggest the bats do in the tunnel that upset the bats?

    A. He suggested they walk the whole way.

    B. He suggested they ride on the backs of the crawlers.

    C. He suggested they stay behind so they didn't slow the group up.

    D. He suggested they fly through the tunnels looking for rats.

Gregor the Overlander

Part 3 Quiz

6. What do rats love?

    A. Themselves.

    B. Food.

    C. Fighting.

    D. Reading.

7. "If you are not trying to hold on to time, you are not so afraid of losing it," tells us Luxa is

    A. an adventurer with lucid thoughts.

    B. envious of Gregor.

    C. very sad.

    D. happy to be on the journey.

8. How did Temp react to Gregor crying about Tick?

    A. She was very angry.

    B. She didn't know what to think.

    C. She was sad.

    D. She was honored.

9. What was wrong with Gregor's father when he was found in the pit?

    A. He acted like a rat.

    B. He didn't want to leave the pit.

    C. He wanted to stay with the rats.

    D. He had a fever.

10. Why was Luxa shocked over Henry's actions at the pit?

    A. He had saved Ripred's life.

    B. Ripred had saved Henry's life.

    C. He had betrayed her to the rats.

    D. He told Luxa he hated Gregor.

Gregor the Overlander

Part 3 Quiz

11. As Gregor confronted the rats at the pits he realized

    A. He really wasn't the warrior.

    B. He was the last to die according to the prophecy.

    C. He wanted to stay in the Underland forever.

    D. Henry would be the last to die.

12. Why did Ares save Gregor instead of Henry?

    A. He liked Gregor more than Henry.

    B. He never liked Henry.

    C. He didn't know Henry was planning to fight with the rats.

    D. He was afraid he would be killed if he didn't save Gregor.

13. What did Gregor's father use to make a compass?

    A. Nothing, he had one in his pocket.

    B. A needle and a bowl of water.

    C. A needle, bowl of water, and lodestone.

    D. A lodestone and a bowl of water.

14. What did Gregor do that shocked the council?

    A. He bonded with Ares.

    B. He screamed and shouted at them for their decision.

    C. He stormed out of the room vowing to never help them again.

    D. He flew off with Ares before anything could be done against Ares.

15. What gift did Vikus tell Gregor he was seeking?

    A. Sandwich's sword.

    B. His father.

    C. Hope.

    D. Faith.

Gregor the Overlander
Part 3 Quiz

16. Why is Gregor concerned about the Prophecy of Bane?

    A. He knows he will have to leave the Overland again.

    B. He realizes he is not the warrior mentioned in it.

    C. He doesn't understand what it means.

    D. He doesn't know if he is mentioned in it.

17. How does Gregor's character grow throughout the book?

    A. He becomes more manipulative.

    B. He cares less and less for Boots.

    C. He becomes more confident in himself.

    D. He becomes arrogant.

18. How did Gregor's father trick the rats into keeping him alive for so long?

    A. He promised them money from the Overland.

    B. He pretended to teach them about science.

    C. Every weapon he made broke after one or two tries.

    D. He promised to show them the way to the Overland.

19. What could most rats do that surprised Gregor?

    A. Write

    B. Read.

    C. Speak to the crawlers.

    D. Make weapons.

20. How could Ripred be characterized?

    A. Dull, slow-witted, and frail.

    B. Intelligent, brave, and dangerous.

    C. Dangerous, dull, and arrogant.

    D. Intelligent, brave, and prudent

Answers to Quizzes

Quiz 1	Quiz Part 2	Quiz Part 3
1. B	1. C	1. D
2. C	2. C	2. A
3. A	3. B	3. A
4. D	4. D	4. C
5. D	5. C	5. B
6. A	6. A	6. A
7. C	7. C	7. C
8. B	8. D	8. D
9. C	9. C	9. D
10. D	10. D	10. C
11. A	11. B	11. B
12. A	12. C	12. C
13. C	13. A	13. C
14. C	14. A	14. A
15. B	15. C	15. C
16. A	16. D	16. D
17. D	17. A	17. C
18. C	18. C	18. C
19. A	19. B	19. B
20. D	20. D	20. B

Made in the USA
Lexington, KY
10 February 2014